Seascape

By

Jannietta

Seascape

ISBN: 978-1-5023-2835-9

©Jannietta 2014

The following poems were first published in Barefoot on Green Grass © 2012
The Orange T Shirt (reworked for this edition), Horizon Line and Dancing with the Dolphins

The poems: Life is Like the Sea, Land of my Belonging and Waves, were fist published in 'Wild Swans Flying' ©2013

Also by Jannietta

Barefoot on Green Grass;

Wild Swans Flying

Arriving: Poems to bring you home

For more information on Jannietta visit her web site:

www.Jannietta.com

To my Husband Ian

Thank you for all the walks by the sea
For all the soul sharing talks and
For always holding my hand
Even when you didn't understand me
And my words fell like whispers over the golden sands

'Love one another, but make not a bond of love;
Let it rather be a moving sea
Between the shore of your souls'
(Kahlil Gibran)

CONTENTS

Life is like the sea

Life is like the sea
it can be fun for a while
playing in the waves
swimming, surfing the breakers
allowing the waves to wash over us
splashing and jumping and sending
their spray into our laughter
But if the waves fail to show
or they disappoint us in some way
it is good to remember
we have the rest of the ocean to enjoy

Waves

Waves break like promises, new and fresh
pounding the shoreline of your life with
a tambourine of sound

Each wave a magnificent thought of God;
an idea whose time is complete.

Now is the time to feel the beat of the tambourine
as it dances in your blood
shaping, sculpting, forming you
form from that which is formless

Now is the time to take the plunge
and ride the waves
Now is the time to save your life
from drowning

Bucket List

To greet each day with a smile
To wonder at my own beauty
To be at peace with how things are
To smile
To laugh
To give generously and listen deeply
To befriend the Great Silence

To dance
To cry
To play
To talk with the trees
Flirt with the flowers
Sing with the ocean
To befriend my enemies

To not get to the end of my life and find I have never
lived it

Barefoot on the sand

Step by step
Loosening
Freeing
Dropping all but the essentials
Of living
Meeting life as it unfolds in the moment
Here and now

This is all there ever is; Heaven and Earth
meeting in mutual embrace
Is anything else ever really needed?

In this moment even the question ceases
To exist

Ancient Stones

*Beneath the gaze of ancient stones
the bare bones of this land speak of beauty*

Beneath the gaze of ancient stones
The bare bones of this land speak of beauty
You enter this landscape alone
Your own solitude moaning inside you

Beneath the gaze of ancient stones
The bare bones of this land are bleeding
Age old stories fill the air with mystery
Returning as waves of prayer on the stony shore

Beneath the gaze of ancient stones
The bare bones of this land are groaning
Remnants of a memory rise up like peace
Pouring through the pores of Mother Earth

This landscape of love will haunt you
You enter alone but you leave owning the wild taste of
wind and wave;
Your bones burning with the desire to return
The song of the ancient stones calling you home

The Land of my Belonging

This is a land of sea and sky
where mournful cries of seagulls swell the air
and a residue of ancient prayer
breathes over the land

This is a land of story
of warrior ways and ancient pathways
of pilgrim hearts and turbulent days
where stillness dwells in the ebb and flow of tide
and a new rhythm of life is born

This is the land of my belonging
into its wild beauty I was called
and named
This land is my homeland
whose timeless mystery
breathes through my veins, like the pulse
of a song, and where
when I walk along the shores of its truth
I know myself differently

Girl on the beach

The young girl sifts the sand for hidden treasures
filling her bucket with reminders of a lost home
remembered but no longer named

The perfect shell, a polished stone, a memory

Like this little girl we too may live our lives
lost in days of dreaming
collecting, sifting
sorting the treasures of our lives
by some criteria we no longer understand,
while all the time unbeknown to us
the daily sand upon which we walk
offers up the name we seek to know

True treasure, it seems, is never where we think it to
be, and besides,
if we could but see
our buckets are already full and over flowing

Pebbles

Smooth, round, softened
caressed into careful shapes, hard
but not hardened, strong
but not resistant

Surely this sculpting is the work of love?

To reshape that which is rough
until it is smooth again
To soften that which has become harsh and hard
To make something loveable out of
that which the world has judged unlovable

In the midst of love all that has been deemed false
must return to truth
and beauty must rise from even the remnants of
despair

In truth all pebbles long to be remade by tenderness
to lay bare their innocence
in one courageous act of surrender

Seagull

On wings of songs unknown
the seagull flies alone
tearing at the heart of memories
held deep in the seas of our
estranged living

There is a strange paradox to life
The longing to be still and the longing to fly
The fear of being free and the fear of being bound
The desire to belong and the desire
to leave the place of belonging
The need to be lost and the need to be found

The need for song and the need for silence

If we had wings we would fly away
yet without them there is no option
but to stay with the longing

True freedom comes
when discovering our hidden wings
we discern how we might use them

The heart of the Ocean

Out walking along the beach
we saw washed up on the sand before us
a softly caressed stone: you called it
"The heart of the ocean"

I took it home and placed it in my peace bowl
where my prayers for love live
It nestled there, at home, safe
amongst the presence of words quietly spoken

In still moments I hear the stone sing
its memory to me:

The sound of the day when eternity
rested in the touch of your hand in mine.
The slow movement of waves
that calmed the world for a while.
The kiss of your smile
awash with breezes from the sea.

Your love the only joy I ever needed.

Seeking

Like waves we arrive on the shore
Many times in a lifetime
Arriving only to leave again
In search of the elusive more
That moves as ocean depth within us

Retreating from the touch of wave
Upon sand
We stand on the shoreline of life
Searching the horizon
Needlessly looking for the waves
That are already here lapping
Around our feet

Blind to the beauty that wants to blind us

Surrender

Let your lips kiss like waves
arriving in the place of belonging
with the fierce tenderness of songs
longing to be sung

Let your caress break like the crescendo of waves
on breathless shoreline; your desire
yielding and opening
to the dance of the sacred sea

Let your touch melt into mine like
shifting sands; our bodies rising
to a new rhythm ; a drum beat
that calls from a different shore

Let our passion pound in our bodies with longings
for ecstasies deep and unknown
Our breath, rise honest like the wind
sighing in total surrender

to the wildness of it all

Dancing with dolphins

Watch as free spirits bathe
bright sunlight caressing
their laughter
warm waters cooling
to the scent of human touch

Mysteries of moon and tide
abandoned, forgotten
salted tears surrender
to sweet azure blue embrace

In timeless wisdom
two species
dance their dreams

Horizon line

The wind blew your words away
stealing them from your lips
before their meaning could settle in my mind
Beyond your shoulders I could see the horizon line
grey sea embracing timeless sky
seagulls squawked their own sad songs
and I thought
"So this is what it's like saying goodbye."

We continued our walk, hands stuffed deep
into coat pockets
fingers curled into clenched fists, fearful
that some strange urge
would send them reaching out for
the familiar touch of yesterday

I turned to look at you
beyond your shoulders the horizon line
blurred
Grey, distant, far away

Song of the wave

Look at me, notice me, watch me,
play with me, admire me, attend to me
see how beautiful I am, how big and strong
how magnificently the ocean moves through me.

See how powerful I am; the King of the Ocean!

It is from the depths of my hidden wildness
that I call to you
From the voice of an unnamed silence that I ask you
to bear witness to my life

Although I may seem loud and brave
in truth I am merely a wave fearing that I may drown
A wave fearing for its own life; wondering
if it is you who has come to save me?

Passion

Waves dance on the shore like flamenco
stirring the deep heat simmering
in the heart of man.
Think crumbled bed linen; the feel of skin
on skin
breathlessness rising.

Only later comes the tenderness we long for,
moonlight kissing the water in still ripples of light.
Love has subsided now; a quiet whisper
waves and ocean meeting in easy recognition
unrestrained and unfettered

Those of us intimate with our own quietness
will feel this freedom; will know
the soft, rippling caress of breath
that is our pathway home

Beached

Lost, confused, forsaken
abandoned and alone
a life of isolation is not a natural way to live

No man is an island; when beached on dry land
his dreams are full of the ocean
his heart yearning for things beyond his reach

'For every thing there is a season
and a time for every purpose under heaven'

Survivors of shipwrecks often speak of miracles

The Orange T Shirt

Walking along the quiet shoreline with
waves running and dancing at my feet
a question rises in my mind
"Where is Life lived?"

From somewhere
(or perhaps from nowhere?)
the answer makes itself known.

"In the spaces; the quiet openings"

Looking around I see
a young girl in an orange T shirt gleefully
riding a donkey, while
on the sidelines her father
returns her joy with a pensive smile

In the sky above a kite dances
joyful and bright; orange too
its colour merges with the surfacing cries
of the wild surfers of the waves

Life is lived here; now
on the edge of a forgotten time
moment by moment I see it all
Life expressing itself

A young girl in an orange T shirt

Seascape

Seascape speaks of spirit and soul
a holy escape from the landscape
of mind driven ways

Why spend our days stuck sinking in the sand, lost in
our limited understanding
when with a little courage
we can swim freely in the ocean depths
and breathe the sanity of
another world?

Shoreline

Sometimes walking the shoreline is difficult
it requires balance, concentration, focus
positioning our feet on the narrow stretch of land
where sea meets shore
involves a steady discipline
one false move and we risk becoming lost at sea
or else remaining forever stranded
on dry land

We may spend lifetimes trying to avoid this place
yet its beauty always commands that we return
for it is only here on the shore of our souls
that we can learn to walk the land
while talking to the water that pours
itself endlessly over our feet

Only on this sacred ground, in this space
can we learn to greet our true nature
with ease and grace
arriving finally to be at peace
with the way things are

Safe Harbour

How will you know the spirit of the open sea
if you never set sail beyond
the harbour walls?
How will you know the thrill of the wild waves
if you never allow yourself to rock the boat?

Storms at sea may betray our security
yet without them we cannot feel
the undercurrent of stillness that rides the waves
or know the peace that hides
in the aftermath of noise

While we stay anchored to the shore
the calm that settles after the storm
will never find us
and without knowing our sorrows
we will never learn to befriend our joys

Life reminds us daily to live wildly
to experience the fullness of the ocean

Playing safe has never been a viable option

Transparency

Who does not love the sight of sunlight dancing
on clear, clean water?
Unspoilt, pure, transparent, bright
even the words themselves hold a healing; a promise
that arrives like a whisper to lie
on the shores of our souls

Speak the words slowly like a sacred mantra.
Hold them, feel them
taste them, touch them

Become the innocence that dances before your eyes

Beneath

So much of life is lived beneath the surface
in a world dark and unknowable
like the unfathomable depths of the ocean floor
where the only light that exists comes from creatures
who illumine the world with their
own inner glow

Scientists have a name for this, they call it
bioluminescence; the ability to shine
from the inside out
It is a useful strategy for warning off predators

For years humans have been diving in the deep seas
yet the lessons found there
rarely surface to see the light of day
and the light of understanding remains slow to dawn
in the closed minds of man

So it remains
that on the surface of life we still fight
our battles with tongue and sword
not knowing that it is the power of our inner light
that is meant to save us

Primal Wave

In each of us there lives a tide of energy
bursting to be known. Mostly we feel it
in the quiet times as longings that
surge onto the shoreline of our lives
with echoes of distant stories; silenced

This is truth seeking a voice; beauty longing to dance
love yearning to feel its own fierceness

This is deep calling to deep

The primal wave seeks out the heart of man
creating for itself a home in the grave
watery shadows
of a world we have yet to understand

Calm

Calm with tranquility
Peace with serenity
Sometimes being lost at sea
Is a beautiful place to be

Storm Damage

Feel for the edges of your life
Go to the farthest shorelines and seek yourself there
amongst the debris that the wild storms
have left behind

You have feared to travel to these places
You have preferred to stay on safer shores
trading the song of sorrows
for the illusions of joy

You have played at living

All the lost fragments of your life lie discarded
on far away shores; unnamed; forgotten;
waiting in agony to be reclaimed

Now is the time to regain your failures
cradle your loneliness, reclaim your despair
make peace with your own ugliness

Storm damage invites you to claim the wreckage
as your own; to give name and home even to
that which it tried to destroy

Gather together the lost fragments of your life
the broken vessels; the pieces of shattered glass
that scatter threats on the ground before you

Now is the time to cut yourself open
even deeper than before
to meet with the vibrant fullness of blood
that courses through your veins
to discover that what you feared would harm you
will complete you

Peace; Be still

Ocean ebbs and flows
The ever changing tide of life
Beyond, beneath, beside, below
Peace breathes a message through the waves

Be still and know

Heron flies across the sea

A heron flies across the surface of the sea
a whisper from the quiet lands beyond

Often we find that very little is needed
for truth to surface
for miracles to make known their gentle ways

So it is that in feeling the flight
of Heron across the water
we might come to touch the days of others
with a quiet love; turning
each moment into a blessing,
a miracle

Learning to see the quiet lands
whispering in the face of others
we might find that a God forsaken world
can be turned back into the paradise
we thought was gone forever

It takes very little for truth to surface

Keep looking for the Heron

Iona Blessing

Spirit of the deep blue sea, bring me courage
Spirit of the dancing waves, bring me joy
Spirit of the untamed ocean, sing to me
Spirit of the moving tides, set me free

Spirit of the rocky shore, bring me strength
Spirit of the timeless sky, grant me peace
Spirit of the bracing winds, breathe in me
Spirit of the ancient land, cradle me

Spirit of this sacred isle
live in me

35482554R00024

Made in the USA
Charleston, SC
10 November 2014